A SONG IN THE NIGHT

Selections from The Spiritual Canticle of Saint John of the Cross

Contents

Acknowledgments

From **The Collected Works of St. John of the Cross,** translated by Kieran Kavanaugh and Otilio Rodriguez © 1979 by Washington Province of Discalced Carmelites., ICS Publications 2131 Lincoln Road, N.E. Washington, D.C. 20002 – for **A Song in the Night** – Selections from **The Canticle of St. John of the Cross.**

Frontispiece; The work of Milo Puiz used here with the permission of Lafayette Carmel, Louisiana.

a Song in the night

Scribed and edited by

Sister Patricia of the Resurrection O.D.C.

Illustrated by Stephen Foster

Biographical notes and introduction to the Spiritual Canticle by
Iain Matthew O.D.C.

published by

SOURCE BOOKS
Trabuco Canyon
California

ANTHONY CLARKE
Wheathampstead
Hertfordshire

First published in Great Britain in 1991 by **Anthony Clarke**,
Wheathampstead, Hertfordshire, England.

First published in the United States of America in 1991 by **Source Books**,
Trabuco Canyon, California.

ISBN 0 85650 105 0 (UK)
ISBN 0 940147 15 7 (USA)

Typesetting by CG Graphics, Aylesbury

Printed and Bound in Great Britain by
Hartnolls Limited, Bodmin, Cornwall.

†

Saint John of the Cross

'His face used to radiate peace and joy – he never appeared depressed, nor vexed with himself or his subjects; he always treated people gently.' So a fellow friar describes St John of the Cross. What was the source of this inner joy?

Certainly not mere absence of pain. John was born into a poor, weaving family in barren Castille in 1542. His father, Gonzalo de Yepes, had been disinherited for marrying beneath him, and John's early years were marked by the affection and penury such a marriage involved. Gonzalo's early death left Catalina, and the two surviving children, Francisco and John, destitute. The mother traipsed from one town to another seeking work, finally settling at Medina del Campo, Castille's international trade centre. Happily, John was received into a school for the poor there – well prepared, then, for the work of his later teens; tending the sick and dying in one of the Medina hospitals. After years spent nursing, begging in the bustling town, studying late at night for classes in the recently founded Jesuit college, John (now 21) came to a mature decision to dedicate his life to God in the Carmelite Order.

His formation as a Carmelite took him to another European centre: the university town of Salamanca, the scene for John of several years of academic and community life, university controversy and cloistered regularity. All set for ordination, crisis ensued: perhaps it was the contrast between the relative comfort of his Salamanca days and his childhood encounter with life's open wounds that made John question his Carmelite life and nerved him to opt for a more severe – Carthusian – existence. He had decided when, in 1567, he met Teresa of Avila: who recognized his spirit, told him of her plans to reform the Carmelite Order, and win him to the cause.

Duruelo, is a hamlet in the Castillian wilderness and it was here that John and three companions inaugurated the life of the Discalced Carmelite friars; a life of intense prayer, simple pastoral care of neighbouring villages and severe poverty. The reform quickly grew and houses of formation were set up.

John was still a young man when he rejoined Teresa in 1572. 'La Madre' had called for him to help her lead the convent of the Incarnation in Avila. There some 180 sisters were demoralized, poor with a poverty not of their choosing and fearful of the talk of reform. John's tact and gentleness had a remarkable effect and the community underwent a profound renewal. But John's presence aggravated those friars who did not share his spirit and in December 1577 the antagonism which reform was creating was unleashed on this simple man. John was kidnapped and taken in secret across the Guadarrama mountains where he was incarcerated in a monastery in Toledo. So began nine months of solitary confinement in a minute dungeon, deprived of light, with inadequate food and few changes of clothes. In the freezing winter and in the stifling heat of summer; the prisoner was allowed out but once a week – to be flogged! In addition to all this went a kind of psychological torture and even the threat of death. And, deep in his spirit, there was affliction even in his relationship with God.

Yet in this confinement, darkness and anguish, (the belly of Jonah's sea-beast; as he was to describe it) John discovered the presence of Christ his Beloved in a way that brought light, freedom and peace: 'the inner resurrection of the spirit'. It is this 'resurrection' that he sings in his poems, composed and written in prison. Among them was the Spiritual Canticle.

John was not only a mystic and a poet; he was also eminently practical, as his captors discovered in mid-August 1578. In most dramatic fashion, during the night, John escaped from the prison and was thus able to rejoin his brethren. He was sent to the relative safety of Andalusia. In the friaries of the south of Spain, John spent ten years; enduring the solitude of the Sierra de Segura; the Inquisition-raided university town of Baeza and the poor monastery overlooking the luxuriant Moorish palace in Granada. Deep prayer and care of his brother and sister Carmelites was coupled with periods of literary activity and extensive travels as Vicar-Provincial. In an age contrasted by the extremes of religious rigorism and total indifference, John stood out because of his personal caring and singular ability to awaken faith.

Back in Castille in 1588, John was nominated to the priory in Segovia. Here began the last and perhaps blackest night for John – yet his love for the Bridegroom turned that night into brilliant day. A major disagreement was developing because the superior was pushing through policies which John considered injurious to the Order and unjust to individuals. At the same time John found himself the victim of a sinister libel campaign, spear-headed by one of his former subjects. The campaign intended to have John thrown out of the reform – the reform he had lived and nearly died for. Against this background, his words reveal their true significance 'Where there is no love, put love, and you will draw out love.'

While this campaign was being waged, John was preparing to carry out his superiors' latest direction: he had been appointed to journey to Mexico. But the 'slight bout of fever' which took him to Ubeda for treatment turned out to be erysipelas – an acute and infectious disease of the skin rivalled only by the pain of the surgery and the aggression of the Prior who resented John's presence. Love, here, did draw out love: as John lay dying, the weeping Prior begged his forgiveness. The scene is a cameo of that admixture of affection and aggression, joy and pain, that John had encountered throughout his life – in which he had learned to recognize 'the night' as the casket 'concealing the hope of day'. He died as one coming home, home to the Bridegroom who had taught him how to live: 'At the evening', John had said, 'you will be examined in love. Learn to love, then, as God wishes.' 14 December 1591.

The Canticle

The *Canticle* has a history. It began as the poetic resonance of John's encounter with his Beloved during his imprisonment at Toledo. There, poetry became the fruit not just of literary skill but of 'love overflowing from mystical understanding'. Originally composed for himself, John's stanzas inspired his fellow Carmelites, inspired and yet perplexed them. They urged him to comment, to write his comments down, and eventually to collect the poetry and prose in a single work, which, after successive redactions by John, comes to us as the 'Spiritual Canticle'.

The phrases from the commentary that follow are not, then, simply wise aphorisms; rather, they are the children of John's heart, sparks from the fire that burned strongly in Toledo, windows onto his own relationship with the Bridegroom. In reading them, we travel from commentary, through poetry, to John's own experience.

The structure of the 'Canticle' is twofold. On the one hand, as we have said, it mirrors the rhythm of John's own spiritual growth: anxious searching – 'Where have you hidden, Beloved?' (Cant 1); enraptured finding – 'My Beloved is the mountains,/ and lonely wooded valleys . . .' (Cant 14-15); deepening communion – 'laying her neck / on the gentle arms of her Beloved' (Cant 22); reciprocal gaze where each is bathed in the Bridegroom's beauty (Cant 36). The central image is, then, bridal union; the biblical inspiration is the Song of Songs; and love, 'the end for which we were created' (Cant 29), is the guiding force.

On this pattern, closest to the poetry and to his own experience, John sets another pattern: the commentary speaks of our, the readers' journey, begun in the Father's plan in the 'day of eternity', ratified 'beneath the tree' in Christ's dying and rising, but fulfilled in our lives only in degrees and gradually. So John speaks of conversion, then initial efforts in the Christian life (Cant 1-12), deeper purification in the state of 'espousal' (13-21), fulfilled communion in the state of 'marriage' (22-40).

John intends his commentary to lead the reader to her own encounter with the Beloved, to find there a window onto her own meaning. So he states in the prologue that his commentary will offer only 'general light', respecting the reader's 'spiritual capacity and individuality'. In turn, he requires of us a taste for beauty, texture, rhythm and silence; understanding will come to us in our turn through 'love, by which divine truths are not only known – they are also experienced.'

In short, the 'Canticle' encapsulates the source of John's joy, and offers it. Christ's love is that source. Ultimately, the texts that follow put us in touch, not only with John, but also with his Master – Christ, the 'deep cavern of the cliff' in whom John comes to rest (Cant 37):

> 'No matter how many mysteries and marvels holy doctors have discovered and saintly souls understood in his life, greater still is that which remains to be said, and even to be understood . . . Christ is like a deep mine, with store upon store of treasures; however deeply we dig, we shall never come to an end.'

Stanzas ~~Between~~ the Soul and the Bridegroom

Bride

1. Where have You hidden,
   Beloved, and left me moaning?
   You fled like the stag
   After wounding me;
   I went out calling You, and You were gone.

2. Shepherds, you that go
   Up through the sheepfolds to the hill,
   If by chance you see
   Him I love most,
   Tell Him that I sicken, suffer, and die.

3. Seeking my Love
   I will head for the mountains and for watersides,
   I will not gather flowers,
   Nor fear wild beasts;
   I will go beyond strong men and frontiers.

4. O woods and thickets
   Planted by the hand of my Beloved!
   O green meadow,
   Coated, bright, with flowers,
   Tell me, has He passed by you?

5. Pouring out a thousand graces,
   He passed these groves in haste;
   And having looked at them,
   With His image alone,
   Clothed them in beauty.

6. Ah, who has the power to heal me?
   Now wholly surrender Yourself!
   Do not send me
   Any more messengers,
   They cannot tell me what I must hear.

7. All who are free
   Tell me a thousand graceful things of You;
   All wound me more
   And leave me dying
   Of, ah, I-don't-know-what behind their stammering.

8. How do you endure
   O life, not living where you live?
   And being brought near death
   By the arrows you receive
   From that which you conceive of your Beloved.

9. Why, since You wounded
   This heart, don't You heal it?
   And why, since You stole it from me,
   Do You leave it so,
   And fail to carry off what You have stolen?

10. Extinguish these miseries,
    Since no one else can stamp them out;
    And may my eyes behold You,
    Because You are their light,
    And I would open them to You alone.

11. Reveal Your presence,
    And may the vision of Your beauty be my death;
    For the sickness of love
    Is not cured
    Except by Your very presence and image.

12. O spring like crystall
    If only, on your silvered-over face,
    You would suddenly form
    The eyes I have desired,
    Which I bear sketched deep within my heart.

Bridegroom

13. Withdraw them, Beloved,
    I am taking flight!
        Return, dove,
    The wounded stag
    Is in sight on the hill,
    Cooled by the breeze of your flight.

Bride

14. My Beloved is the mountains,
    And lonely wooded valleys,
    Strange islands,
    And resounding rivers,
    The whistling of love-stirring breezes,

15. The tranquil night
    At the time of the rising dawn,
    Silent music,
    Sounding solitude,
    The supper that refreshes, and deepens love.

16. Catch us the foxes,
    For our vineyard is now in flower,
    While we fashion a cone of roses
    Intricate as the pine's;
    And let no one appear on the hill.

17. Be still, deadening north wind;
    South wind come, you that waken love,
    Breathe through my garden,
    Let its fragrance flow,
    And the Beloved will feed amid the flowers.

18. You girls of Judea,
    While among flowers and roses
    The amber spreads its perfume,
    Stay away, there on the outskirts:
    Do not so much as seek to touch our thresholds.

19. Hide Yourself, my Love;
    Turn Your face toward the mountains,
    And do not speak;
    But look at those companions
    Going with her through strange islands.

Bridegroom 20. Swift-winged birds,
    Lions, stags, and leaping roes,
    Mountains, lowlands, and river banks,
    Waters, winds, and ardors,
    Watching fears of night:

21. By the pleasant lyres
    And the siren's song, I conjure you
    To cease your anger
    And not touch the wall,
    That the bride may sleep in deeper peace.

22. The bride has entered
    The sweet garden of her desire,
    And she rests in delight,
    Laying her neck
    On the gentle arms of her Beloved.

23. Beneath the apple tree:
    There I took you for My own,
    There I offered you My hand,
    And restored you,
    Where your mother was corrupted.

Bride 24. Our bed is in flower,
    Bound round with linking dens of lions,
    Hung with purple,
    Built up in peace,
    And crowned with a thousand shields of gold.

25. Following Your footprints
    Maidens run along the way;
    The touch of a spark,
    The spiced wine,
    Cause flowings in them from the balsam of God.

26. In the inner wine cellar
    I drank of my Beloved, and, when I went abroad
    Through all this valley
    I no longer knew anything,
    And lost the herd which I was following.

27. There He gave me His breast;
    There He taught me a sweet and living knowledge;
    And I gave myself to Him,
    Keeping nothing back;
    There I promised to be His bride.

28. Now I occupy my soul
    And all my energy in His service;
    I no longer tend the herd,
    Nor have I any other work
    Now that my every act is love.

29. If, then, I am no longer
    Seen or found on the common,
    You will say that I am lost;
    That, stricken by love,
    I lost myself, and was found.

30. With flowers and emeralds
    Chosen on cool mornings
    We shall weave garlands
    Flowering in Your love,
    And bound with one hair of mine.

31. You considered
    That one hair fluttering at my neck;
    You gazed at it upon my neck
    And it captivated You;
    And one of my eyes wounded You.

32. When You looked at me
    Your eyes imprinted Your grace in me;
    For this You loved me ardently;
    And thus my eyes deserved
    To adore what they beheld in You.

33. Do not despise me;
    For if, before, You found me dark,
    Now truly You can look at me
    Since You have looked
    And left in me grace and beauty.

Bridegroom

34. The small white dove
    Has returned to the ark with an olive branch;
    And now the turtledove
    Has found its longed-for mate
    By the green river banks.

35. She lived in solitude,
    And now in solitude has built her nest;
    And in solitude He guides her,
    He alone, Who also bears
    In solitude the wound of love.

Bride

36. Let us rejoice, Beloved,
    And let us go forth to behold ourselves in your beauty,
    To the mountain and to the hill,
    To where the pure water flows,
    And further, deep into the thicket.

37. And then we will go on
    To the high caverns in the rock
    Which are so well concealed;
    There we shall enter
    And taste the fresh juice of the pomegranates.

38. There You will show me
    What my soul has been seeking,
    And then You will give me,
    You, my Life, will give me there
    What You gave me on that other day:

39. The breathing of the air,
    The song of the sweet nightingale,
    The grove and its living beauty
    In the serene night,
    With a flame that is consuming and painless.

40. No one looked at her,
    Nor did Aminadab appear;
    The siege was still;
    And the cavalry,
    At the sight of the waters, descended.

a Song
in the night

How do you pray?

I look on God's
beauty
and rejoice that
He possesses
it.

Mother Francisca's answer to John of the Cross'
question — " How do you pray?"   (1)

Faith and Love

are like a blind man's guide.
They will lead you
        along a path unknown
        to you —
        to the place where
God is Hidden.

cf. Cant. 1/11   (2)

Always
regard Him
as Hidden —
Serve Him
in Secret.

Cant 1/12   (3)

He has
made
darkness
his
Hiding place.

cf. Psalm 17:12 (4)

The truly
loving heart
is content with
nothing less
than
His Presence.

Come,

even into your secret room,
shut the door behind you,
hide yourself
a little
even for a moment.

cf Cant 1 — Is. 26:20   (6)

You yourself
are His
Dwelling
His secret room
t
Hiding place.

one of the outstanding favours
God grants briefly in this life is:

An understanding and experience
of Himself
so lucid
so lofty
as to make one know clearly
that He can NEVER
be completely understood
or experienced

cf. Cant 7   (8)

Why search elsewhere
when within you
you possess
/your riches
delights
satisfaction
fullness
+
Kingdom
Your Beloved

Whom you desire
+ seek.

cf. Cant 1/8   (9)

Love
is paid
only with
Love
itself

Cant 9   (10)

Such is the truly loving heart:

like a hungry man
    craving for food

like a sick person
    moaning for health

like one suspended in the
    air

    with nothing to lean on.

Loves'
work
is Love

of this work
the lover awaits
its perfection
and completion

Cant 9   (12)

Become aware
of Wisdom's Harmony –
the created world
will become
for you
a Symphony———

In all creation
He has left some
trace of who He is.

In looking upon them
He has clothed them
with his beauty.

cf Cant 5   (14)

over the sketch
of faith
is drawn

the will
of the
lover.

TRUE LOVE

receives all things that come
from the Beloved

well being
trouble
reproach

with the same evenness of soul,
since they are
His Will.

among lovers
the wound of
one
is a wound
for both,
and the two
have but
one
feeling.

Cant 13 (17)

*

Awakened love
is like a falling
stone —

rushing to its centre.

* *

Awakened love
is like wax in which
an impression is being
made

but is not yet complete.

* * *

Awakened love
is like a
sketch
or first draft

it calls out to the artist:
Complete
your
work!

Love of God is your soul's real health. You will not enjoy full health 'till Love is complete in you.

As each
sings His
praise differently
All
together

form a symphony
of
LOVE.

He is
Silent
Music
and
Sounding
Solitude

Cant 14/15   (21)

Tell the Beloved,

I am sick - he is my health.
I am suffering - he is my joy
I am near death

   He alone is my life —

Give me health, joy, life.

South
you that waken
love
Wind

breathe through my garden
Let its fragrance flow.

Cling
to him
for in this
life
consists.

Deut. 30:20   (24)

When God looks

he loves ...

by this look of love He makes the beloved
gracious and pleasing to Himself.

Cant 32　　(25)

" They have no wine."...
" Lazarus whom you love is sick."...

The discreet lover
doesn't ask
for what she lacks

but only indicates
the need _

So that the Beloved
may do what He
pleases _____

cf. Cant 1   (26)

God makes use
of NOTHING other than
LOVE

all our works
all our trials

are nothing in the sight of God _
He has no need of these things
for there is no way He can exalt
the soul more - than by making
her equal with Himself.

He is pleased only with her
LOVE

Cant 28   (27)

Nothing
is
obtained
from God
except
by

Love

cf. Cant 1/13 (28)

When God is
loved
He very readily
answers
the requests of
His
Lover

cf Caut 1/12 (29)

A little
of pure
love

is more precious to God,
to the soul,
and more beneficial to the
Church —

than all other works put
together.

Cant 29   (30)

When a faint
light is mingled
with a bright one —
the bright light
prevails
+ it is that which
illumines

Cant 26   (31)

God never
judges a thing
twice
once He has blotted
out
sin and ughiness
there is no reproach

The power and tenacity
of Love
is great

for love captures and
binds
God Himself

God's gaze

cleanses
endows with grace
enriches
and illumines
like the sun that dries and
provides warmth and beauty
and splendour when it
pours down its rays.

cf. Cant 33   (34)

I
Shall lead
her
into solitude
and
there
Speak to her heart.

Osee 2:16   (35)

Having travelled a long journey
the first thing a person wants
to do is to see and speak with
the Beloved.

The first thing the soul wants
upon coming to the vision of
God is to know and enjoy
the deep and secret mysteries
of the Incarnation and the
ancient ways of God
dependent upon it.

A true desire
    for WISDOM
seeks suffering first.

It enters WISDOM
by the thicket of the
            CROSS

Eye
has not seen
nor
ear heard
nor has it entered
your
heart
What the Beloved
has
prepared
for you.

Love's Lesson

It is as if He were to put an instrument in the Beloved's hands & shows her how it works by operating it jointly with her.

He shows her how to
love
+
gives the ability to do so.

The Wedding gifts of the Beloved †

to receive the crown of life
to eat from the tree of life
to be given the hidden manna
to discover the white stone
to be a pillar in the temple
to have power over the nations
to be called the morning star
to be clothed in white
to hear my own new name
to be called by a secret name
to bear the name of the city
to bear the name of God

cf. Cant 38

(40)

Oh, Soul!

Created for such gifts
and called to them!

WHAT ARE YOU DOING?
HOW ARE YOU SPENDING YOUR
TIME?

You are blind to such a
light
Deaf to such a loud
call.

cf. Cant. 39   (41)

Prayer of John t

may the most Sweet Jesus
be pleased
to bring all who invoke
His Name

to this glorious marriage.

cf. Cant 40   (42)

References

1 cf Collected Works (hereafter referred to as K/R) p. 400

2 cf K/R p. 420

3 cf K/R p. 420

4 cf K/R p. 421
also cf p. 37 of General Introduction on St. John's translation of scriptural passages.

5 cf K/R p. 436

6 cf K/R p. 419

7 cf K/R p. 418

8 cf K/R p. 440

9 cf K/R p. 419

10 cf K/R p. 444

11 cf K/R p. 444

12 cf K/R p. 445

13 cf K/R p. 472

14 cf K/R pp. 434, 435

15 cf K/R p. 455

16 cf K/R p. 451

17 cf K/R p. 460

18 cf K/R p. 453

19 cf K/R p. 452

20 cf K/R p. 473

21 cf K/R pp. 472, 473

22 cf K/R p. 427

23 cf K/R p. 478 Stanza 17

24 cf Deut. 30:20 cf note 4 above

25 cf K/R p. 535

26 cf K/R p. 427

27 cf K/R p. 520

28 cf K/R p. 421

29 cf K/R p. 421

30 cf K/R p. 523

31 cf K/R p. 515

32 cf K/R p. 537

33 cf K/R p. 534

34 cf K/R p. 537

35 cf Osee 2:4, K/R p. 543

36 cf K/R p. 550

37 cf K/R p. 549

38 cf K/R p. 555

39 cf K/R p. 554

40 cf K/R p. 555ff.

41 cf K/R p. 559

42 cf K/R p. 565

99

The Desert—— shall——— ———blossom

The Ideals and Traditions of the Carmelites

A short collection of essays on the character and purpose of the order, its ideals and history and its development in Britain today.

Throughout the pages of this small book readers will get an insight into the particular Christian *vision* that has guided Carmelites down the ages and still is theirs as, with everyone else, they move with time forwards towards the enigmatic future.

32pp   ISBN 0 85650 067 4   *Paperback*

Fr. MALACHY LYNCH ★ ★

first Prior of the Return.

The Sanctuary at Aylesford, dedicated to the Assumption of the Glorious Virgin

A Directory of Monastic Hospitality

Edited by the Commission on the Economics of the Contemplative Life.

The Directory provides detailed information concerning hospitality offered by the monasteries, both Catholic and Anglican, in the United Kingdom. Included are forty six Convents and Monasteries of nuns and thirty two monasteries of monks.

84pp   ISBN 0 85650 045 2   *Paperback*

Published by **ANTHONY CLARKE**

The Life of
SAINT TERESA OF ÁVILA
by Elizabeth Hamilton

Originally published under the title *The Great Teresa* the author has succeeded in providing her readers with a portrait of one of the Church's greatest saints and doctors. The detail of attention to all aspects of Saint Teresa's life has gained such appreciation as G.B. Stern's in *The Catholic Herald* who wrote, "One has nothing but praise for her vital recreation of a saint who might otherwise, because of her very greatness, be in danger of seeming too much of a mystic to be human."

A full index detailed bibliography of Saint Teresa's own writings and other relevant works and also a useful chronology of the main events in her life complete this outstanding book.　　　　192pp　ISBN 0 85650 064 X　*Paperback*

THE
STORY
OF A
SOUL

The Autobiography of Saint Thérèse of Lisieux

Translated by Michael Day, Cong. Orat.

The autobiography writing of St. Thérèse of Lisieux edited by her sister Mother Agnes of Jesus, and published under the title: *The Story of a Soul*, have exercised a profound influence on Christian spirituality during the last century.

In a critical preface to his translation Father Michael Day explains the circumstances in which *The Story of a Soul* was first given to the world, the details of its composition and of the editorial work carried out, at the Saint's request, by Mother Agnes.　　　　192pp　ISBN 0 85650 026 7　*Paperback*

Saint Thérèse of Lisieux
A LIFE OF SISTER THERESE OF THE CHILD JESUS FOR CHILDREN
CHRISTINE FROST　ILLUSTRATED BY ELIZABETH OBBARD ODC

ISBN 0 85650 081 X　*Paperback*

Bernadette of Lourdes
By Frances Parkinson Keyes

In the anguish of the world today the story of "the sublime shepherdess" is the comfort and inspiration of millions of the faithful who greatly hope and trust in the compassion of the Queen of Heaven, who chose as bearer of her message a peasant girl whose humility was modelled on her own.　　　　ISBN 0 85650 030 5　*Paperback*

Published by ANTHONY CLARKE

"I have led you into the land of Carmel, to feast on its best and its finest fruits" (Jer. 2:7)

CARMELITE MONASTERIES OF GREAT BRITAIN

BIRKENHEAD	Grosvenor Pl., Birkenhead, Merseyside L43 1UA
BRANKSOME	St. Aldhelm's Rd., Branksome, Poole, Dorset BH13 6BS
CHICHESTER	Hunston Rd,, Chichester, Sussex PO20 6NP
DARLINGTON	Nunnery Lane, Darlington, Co. Durham DL3 9PN
DOLGELLAU	Cader Rd., Dolgellau, Gwynedd LL40 1SH Wales
DUMBARTON	17, Helenslee Rd., Dumbarton G82 4AN Scotland
DYSART	Dysart, Fife KY1 2TF Scotland
FALKIRK	3, Arnothill, Falkirk, Stirlingshire FK1 5RZ Scotland
GLASGOW	29, Mansionhouse Rd., Langside, Glasgow G41 3DN Scotland
GOLDERS GREEN	119, Bridge Lane, Golders Green, London NW11 9JT
KIRKINTILLOCH	Waterside, Kirkintilloch, Glasgow G66 3PE Scotland
LANGHAM	Langham, Holt, Norfolk NR25 7BP
LANHERNE	St. Mawgan, Newquay, Cornwall TR8 4ER
LIVERPOOL	Honeysgreen Lane, Liverpool L12 9HY
MANCHESTER	Vine Street, Salford M7 0PS
NOTTING HILL	P.O. Box 624, St. Charles' Square, London W10 6EA
OBAN	Rockfield Rd., Oban, Argyll PA34 5DQ Scotland
PRESTON	St. Vincent's Rd., Fulwood, Preston, Lancs. PR2 4QA
QUIDENHAM	Quidenham, Norwich, Norfolk NR16 2PH
READING	1, Southcote Rd., Reading RG3 2AD
SCLERDER	Sclerder, Near Looe, Cornwall PL13 2JD
SHEFFIELD	Kirk Edge, High Bradfield, Sheffield S6 6LJ
ST. HELENS	Green Lane, Eccleston, St. Helens, Merseyside WA10 5HH
TAVISTOCK	1 Watts Rd., Tavistock, S. Devon PL19 8LF
UPHOLLAND	Upholland, Skelmersdale, Lancs WN8 0QE
WARE	Ware Park, Ware, Herts. SG12 0DT
WETHERBY	Wood Hall, Linton, Wetherby, West Yorks LS22 4HZ
WOLVERHAMPTON	Poplar Rd., Penn Fields, Wolverhampton WV3 7DP
YORK	Thicket Priory, York YO4 6DE

Published by **PRESTON CARMEL** *– extract from* **The Land of Carmel**